REFUSAL

REFUSAL

POEMS

Jenny Molberg

LOUISIANA STATE UNIVERSITY PRESS ▌▌▌ BATON ROUGE

Published by Louisiana State University Press
Copyright © 2020 by Jenny Molberg
All rights reserved
Manufactured in the United States of America
LSU Press Paperback Original
First printing

DESIGNER: *Mandy McDonald Scallan*
TYPEFACE: *Whitman*
PRINTER AND BINDER: *LSI*

Library of Congress Cataloging-in-Publication Data

Names: Molberg, Jenny, 1985– author.
Title: Refusal : poems / Jenny Molberg.
Description: Baton Rouge : Louisiana State University Press, [2020]
Identifiers: LCCN 2019040517 (print) | LCCN 2019040518 (ebook) | ISBN
    978-0-8071-7074-8 (paperback) | ISBN 978-0-8071-7344-2 (pdf) | ISBN
    978-0-8071-7345-9 (epub)
Subjects: LCGFT: Poetry.
Classification: LCC PS3613.O445 R44 2020 (print) | LCC PS3613.O445
    (ebook) | DDC 811/.6—dc23
LC record available at https://lccn.loc.gov/2019040517
LC ebook record available at https://lccn.loc.gov/2019040518

for all writers of unsent letters

—

and for my mother the conqueror

And this drive to self-knowledge, for woman, is more than a search for identity: it is part of her refusal of the self-destructiveness of male-dominated society.

   —ADRIENNE RICH, "When We Dead Awaken: Writing as Re-Vision," 1972

"Once more, why this refusal?" he asked.

". . . If I were to marry you, you would kill me. You are killing me now."

His lips and cheeks turned white—quite white.

"I SHOULD KILL YOU—I AM KILLING YOU? Your words are such as ought not to be used: violent, unfeminine, and untrue."

   —CHARLOTTE BRONTË, *Jane Eyre*

CONTENTS

i.

Note

He said he would hang himself
so as not to make a mess.

But he was still there the next day.
And the next. And the next.

He wrote the note for the cops
on a page he tore from my favorite book

of poems. That's all I saw of it—
in absence—the ripped-out page

like a jagged fin down the spine.
What is my body but a rainstorm?

What are my bones
but flightless shards of light?

I did not feel secure,
though I married the only man

I believed was safe. Two children.
Three dogs. The dying cat.

Papers signed and unsigned.
The woman who pasted her face

over mine in our photos
and mailed them as proof of their affair

before she tried to kill herself.
This, too, he does not tell me.

In the dream, he cuts
the air around my body

with a giant pair of scissors,
origamis me   .

until I am small as a ring box.
In I go, with the rest

of my clothes, to the cardboard crate
where dress-sleeves stick out

like the arms of paper dolls. I nestle there.
I fold and fold. I try to disappear.

Epistle from the Hospital for Cheaters

to C.C.

What to do with all this flame but douse it
with paper cups of red and yellow pills?
What to do with the sun that licks its rose blaze
across the tiled corners of this ward,
with all these hours, with the burden of relief
we're allowed to feel? We still breathe.
We still walk the halls in our spoiled bodies.
Once, we made a promise in that world
of papers and rings and aisles
that meant *cold prison cell*, that meant
debt and *paranoia* and *many small failings*
that took root as we stood in front of judges
and priests, our teeth crawling with *'til death*.
Gold light razors the plastic blinds.
Don't we look so flawed, so lovely? *Alone forever*
doesn't mean shit anymore. *Tell me*
I didn't blow up my life for this means you get
dark chocolate and a long hug. The food here
is delicious, and we're all going to be fine.
Here, no one cuts your face out of all the photos.
There are no photos. We won't remember this place.
Here, we redefine *slut* as *person who survived*.
When we really hurt, they give us neon casts
for all the broken promises. We sign them like yearbooks.
The IVs drip wine. In the evenings, we play hearts
and watch the sun set on the green
and think doesn't that look like an egg
descending a blue tube of sky. One of us holds
that sun on her tongue awhile. She wants a child,
but not her husband's child. Never her husband's child.

The Wolf of Coole Park

On our honeymoon, my new husband
says he misses his children,
wants to go home. The green hills
vanish like animal eyes closing in the dark
of the park's constant drizzle.
I am not proud of my anger
but a lie can turn the body inside out.

My collected Yeats is getting wet
and I hold it inside my shirt like a pistol.
We pass a stone inscribed:
the bell-beat of their wings above my head—
the absence in my belly is the lake's gray lack
of swans, though I think I see something
white and ruffled on the far shore.

The wind, knocking love loose.
I walk the path into the Seven Woods,
wanting to be lost. But he catches up.
Then, in the distance, a gunshot—

a growl thickens within the trees.
Did you hear that? he says. *Yes*
I say, and think *all is lost between us.*
I will leave him standing there,
will always follow this hungry phantom
deeper into the woods.

Epistle from the Hospital for Text Messaging

to T.B.

I have made of myself a rabbit.
I can no longer speak. Language

is only the *click click click* of my heart
ticking faster now.

I stepped out of my dress.
I autofilled myself. I slipped

the gray skins over my head.
I know you love to watch the animal

of me, my fast-pounding brain.
How I enter the garden

to pluck berries with my teeth,
then the (. . .) (. . .) (. . .) of my leaving.

I know you love to watch the end
of me. I vanish beyond the field

whose borders I built
with your thousand barbed unsaids.

I vanish into the sky.
I vanish into the moon,

this lemon slice of dead volcano.
Here I wait, my fingerless ears

poised as satellites, projecting my rabbit-
shaped silence on space's blank walls.

Something I don't understand about myself
makes people want to hurt me.

Said the Poet

You are a frozen pond with fish pulsing beneath Look in the mirror Say you're beautiful Why don't you touch me more Why are you holding yourself I killed the only pet I ever loved This isn't yelling This isn't my definition of yelling My own father yells until my mother is silent as a sea cave Asleep you are my bird underground in a box I want to touch all your feathers I swear I'll be better Wake up Your friends don't love you Your family doesn't love you I am a good person I am a good poet Once I stood on the train tracks too long I am the victim here I didn't sleep with that student Marry me I hated you last night Be the mother of my children I have a very good reputation My childhood was dappled with henbit Why won't you open the door Why aren't you answering me You should be ashamed of yourself You are a cricket I am the light Be with me forever Why are you afraid Get down on your knees and say you're sorry Have another drink Take off your clothes Try getting angry It feels so good

The List

The forest opened and there was a table
with tea sandwiches and a bright red kettle
and God said, *have a seat.* I had been lost
in the woods a long time, running
from the man who was trying to kill me. I kept
wanting to turn back, until I made
so many circles I didn't recognize my own feet.
All the trees had changed. Now I believed
what he'd said; I was crazy, cruel, a child.
With feet like fish in the silver light,
I stepped around the bodies of deer,
strewn across the forest floor as apples.
I did not look at the yellow wolves
that fed on them.

                                    God said
I know you love to read. Her hair was short
and she had the gray eyes of my sister.
I know how you love language, she said as she
poured some tea. The cup was not chipped.
When I looked through the leaves I saw
the faces of the children I thought I would have
with the man who could not love me.
God handed me some paper. *Make a list,*
she said. *After each number, write "I am."*

                                    God said
Your self is your context. You know the definitions;
you've read every page. Her eyes
were moons of invisible planets.
I was ready to read my list aloud
but God would not let me.
Cross out number 5, she said.
An arrow landed in my heart.
5. I am a good friend, I had written.
The forest narrowed and around the edges
of my sight a blackness crept in.

Can anyone do this to you? God asked me.
Are you going to let a man do this to you?
Cross out number 8, she said.
8. I deserve to be loved.
I could not speak for the pain in my chest.
Who is going to do this to you?
She was beginning to shout. *Who?*

After Pawning the Engagement Ring

I go to the museum and sit before Robert Motherwell's
Elegy to the Spanish Republic with three black holes in my head.
One for the way I hated the poet when he called me stupid.
Another black hole because I felt like a child, carsick
and chicken. *I don't care what day it is,* he said on my birthday.
Was he an aperture, opening inside me?
Or was he a bullet I must dodge for the rest of my life?
At the Cash America Pawn, I waited in line, the ring box
white as ivory, a severed tusk singeing a hole through my hand.

One more black hole, there, in the middle. The question
I asked in my head for a year: How can he think
he owns other people? Him, in the dark, calling my body
his. My breasts, my hair, my hips. I shout *leave*
into Motherwell's circles. I know I can't help it, the ring
in its strange case, cold as a head with no body.

Epistle from the Ruins

to K.H.

Today we tour the ancient Roman ruins
that lie beneath the hospital's wing for young mothers.
Needless to say, the tour guide tells us, the hospital
has been here a long time, since the days they had to reattach
the heads of many patients, or wrap their limbs
in fish scales until the skin grew back. Before we descend,
we pass around a splinter of a singed stake.
We take the elevator down a tunnel lined with shards
of old statues and placards, but only one of us,
the grandmother, can read the lettering.
We move into the wine-making chamber. Stems and seeds
were collected in a stone tub; the women sat
on decorated columns, peeling skin from purple fruit.
In the fermentation vats, we notice rivers
of hairpin cracks in the old terra cotta, how they swell
from the ground, round and immovable as tumors.
Finally, the ancient laundry, where we crush leaves
of woad in our palms; they dye our hands blue.
We inhale strands of saffron, then shred them,
recognizing our own small powers. As a souvenir,
we each receive a white rock crystal. *This is your virginity,*
our tour guide tells us, *Kiss it anytime for good luck.*

Epistle from the Henares River

Still I can hear it: in Spain, the sound
of a man hating me so loud. He invented new sounds

tearing through our apartment, conducting
his own anger. Storks made throat-sounds

like brass knuckles against bone. I startled through rooms,
a spooked horse. This was the sound

of me becoming what I wasn't. Scared thing. Liar.
My mother's voice on the phone: the only sound

I could take. I was afraid to say
what was happening to me. Her plain-sounds

5,000 miles gone. Me, listening. The headphone cord,
roped around my neck, sounding

its split-reined hymns in my ears. *Call the police.*
This is how you call the police in Spain: 112. Sounds

of hooves in her voice. He began to put his hands on me
and she made a little sound,

trying to listen. Then, no sound.
This is how you command a horse, sounds

calm, low: *whoa, whoa.* So when I was pinned
and he ripped the headphones from my ears, the sound

of my mother's voice clattered against the hardwood,
a child falling down a well. A sound

that haunted my dreams for years: *Jenny, Jenny—*
an Atlantic away, my mother's futile sounds.

Epistle from the Hospital for Evolution

to T.B.

There was once a woman, we've learned,
who became a leopard's dinner.

There was once a woman, we've also learned,
who escaped while the leopard ate her sister.

She waded into the ocean, her child
in her arms, until the leopard grew tired

of his hydrophobia. Most of the hair
fell from her body. She discovered

a rock and anvilled open clams. Like the blue
whale, beneath her skin grew a layer of fat.

Here, we take night swims,
go to bed with wet hair. The hospital literature

destroys the Mighty Hunter with his fires
and his bipedal nonsense. We all work

toward degrees in marine biology.
Breakfast is fish and fruit and no one

says a word in prayer circle, but we can all hear.
We learn how to use our fins again.

Some nights, a patient tells her story.
While she speaks her vibrations

we hold our breath and her language
dives beneath our skin and settles there.

All we ever lose is salt, which we will
drink again, which makes us lighter.

The Love Song of Demogorgon

Hither the sound has borne us—to the realm
of Demogorgon, and the mighty portal . . .
—SHELLEY, *Prometheus Unbound*

Love is the world reversed. Nothing but a scribble
in a drizzling cave. Good Christians

do not speak my name but still I rise inside
your body, slither amphibian from your lips.

Don't look at me. I'm chaos—
despite the bit of earth left in me,

I resemble nothing. Face like a starfish.
Fingers like rodents in flight. My mind

made of two minds, I change.
Two-headed ruler of a twofold world.

The higher mind flays me, that shadow box
I play inside—I, its mean puppet,

moving by night. Come for me
with your nail-studded bat.

I will make you do the most terrible things.

Ophelia Rolls the Twenty-Sided Die

1. I do not know, my lord, what I should think.
2. I shall obey, my lord.
3. To speak of horrors,—he comes before me.
4. My lord, I do not know; / But truly, I do fear it.
5. He took me by the wrist and held me hard . . .
6. I did repel his fetters and denied / His access to me.
7. My lord?
8. Could beauty, my lord, have better commerce than with honesty?
9. Indeed, my lord, you made me believe so.
10. I was the more deceived.
11. . . . O, woe is me, / To have seen what I have seen, see what I see!
12. No, my lord.
13. Aye, my lord.
14. 'Tis brief, my lord.
15. Still better, and worse.
16. The king rises.
17. How should I your true love know / From another one?
18. He is dead and gone; At his head a grass-green turf, / At his heels a stone.
19. Pray you, mark.
20. And will he not come again? And will he not come again?

Epistle from the Hospital for Laundry

to J.M.B.

I like it when you do my laundry, the poet used to say,
it makes me feel loved. If only I would touch
him more, he would add. That made him feel loved too,

I tell the doctor this morning as she scribbles
in her yellow pad, her shirt hot-white and starched.
I couldn't tell you what made me feel loved,

or whether anyone asked. Once, in Barcelona, I walked
the mosaiced floors of an ancient Roman laundry,
underground, because years are a slow avalanche

that bury the past and the people in it.
I didn't mean to put the shirts in the wrong drawer,
I thought, walking the sunken halls alone.

Traces of indigo on the dyeing workshop's walls
rolled their little painted eyes at me.
When I didn't feel like touching, I tell the doctor,

I did it anyway. I was at the laundry alone
because the poet had left me. He kept coming back
then leaving, then coming back. What was it Wilbur said

in his poem about laundry? *The soul shrinks . . .*
from the punctual rape of every bléssed day.
For months I dreamt of folding clothes.

The shirts bloomed with wine and blood,
multiplying, mountaining, until
I'd learned to survive my own burial.

Eating Alone

Barcelona

Hija she says *eres triste*
and her hands work my neck
my shoulders my calves my feet
I'm eating poke by the sea
salmon pink as tongues
watermelony cubes of tuna
mangoes slipping like gossip
through my chopsticks
I've been alone so long
I'd welcome anyone's
hands around my neck
For one the waiter says
and sits me in the corner
Even the accordionist
avoids my gaze
The gazpacho is thickened
with day-old baguette
a plate of the tiniest squares
of cucumber tomato onion
I roll them like dice
into the cold soup
Amor de Amarillo the bartender calls me
Does he mean yellow or gold
Does he mean amber
Does he mean I have value
I am not a lemon
I am not a canary though I am
often taken into dark caves
Is anyone waiting
for me to stop singing
Is anyone waiting for me
to rise from the ground
I'm not gold
maybe I am thickened resin
Here is my heart preserved
Here is my self made of tree

At the Bar del Pla I'm allowed
a little seat a little food
The couple next to me never
stops kissing
I try the white wine with bonito
I try the red thunder in a glass
with the octopus bomb
Something ticks inside me
The girls at the next table keep
looking and laughing
After you, everything
tastes like a bruise

Turbine

My husband hated trees—
        trees'd come up on the street sides,
he'd shudder.
        Trees as far as my eyes go.
And up the radio.
        And up all the windows.
Evergreens were the worst—
        how they banded
the horizon that gleamed
        like a hatchet between the limbs.
I might well
        be going on, I'd think,
be never coming back.
        And the windmills on I–69:
they cut the sky to shreds.
        Open air,
that's all he wanted.
        Flat lines.

The Night I Left

I said goodbye to the boys'
boyless rooms and the stuffed animals
blinked their plastic eyes,
folded their muppet arms.
The towel shaped like a monkey
bowed its flimsy head, the ghost
of a child still dampening its matted chest.
I'm sorry, I said to the towel.
I'm sorry, I said to the monster
their mother had knit in blue yarn.

I'm so sorry, I said to the cat
who sounded his soundless mew,
leapt from the bed, and skulked
out of the room. I turned off the lights.
Years passed. Then I was this woman
saying *I'm sorry, I'm so sorry*
until it meant nothing, and someone else
came to carry me to bed.

ii.

Epistle from the Hospital for Emily Post's Wedding Gift Return Etiquette

to M.G.

My mother at my wedding was desert rose
in all its gypsum unfurling, pink and gold,

wanting me, I know, to be happy
more than I ever did. My mother

always says *I'm only as happy*
as my least happy child

so I can't imagine when I will stop
saying I'm sorry. She placed the peonies

in crosshatches of the wrought-
iron wedding arch.

She cued the slideshow.
She told the guitarist where to set up

and apologized, I'm sure, for the hot sun
that ignited the wooden deck.

Steamed the men's suits,
readjusted the necklaces, tasted

the cake, helped the grandmothers
to their seats.

Now as I begin
to go to pieces, I try to see us

as a two-dimensional plane:
woman and grown daughter,

her hand on my bent back,
how we extend beyond—

Epistle in Utero

to P.M.

I unborn you feathered
hair you roller skates you
cheerleader you posing
trellis lace white
crop top you cut-offs
one day you know me
you love me more than you
you marry
he blonde hair he
doctor he smart hands
like blocks he careful
hands sometimes you angry
most times you love and love
you plant pink flowers
you beat eggs he eats
he is long walks he learns
owl calls screech owls swoop
all the trees like you
he hears your voice
in screech above
I born you hear me
cry I grow up I grow old
you love and love me well
you are a well you
at the hospital I need help
I will need you
like you I love too much
I love and it hurts you cold
compress you feel
powerless I across an ocean
one day I am an ocean
in you one day I am an ocean
one day you try to forget
I am here you take care
of me one day I will be
one day you love me
more than you love you

Hippocampus

To the child, you're a stranger, wearing the clothes
of her mother. You are tired at church

and your breath whispers its sour cherries
and burnt sativa into small, obedient ears.

Beneath your ruffled cardigan you wear your arm
in a homemade sling. Another dreamless sleep.

The hippocampus (Greek: seahorse) is the memory's
lockbox, nestled in the brain's coralline folds.

Each time you black out, the little foal
curls inward, refuses retrospection.

A grape-colored landscape paints itself
across your collarbone. Last night, after you fell,

the dog could not lick you awake, and whined
to the tune of the china cabinet, still quaking.

Is this a matter of memory?
Your mind sets loose your addled

stampedes and only the heart can shepherd them
back to their stables. Moving through

the pews, you're a ghost of the woman I knew,
you're hydromedusa, translucent hands reaching

for holy water. You kneel beside the child (me).
She opens her mouth; she receives the wine.

Inside the wet pitch of your headache,
a doused, curved, hooved thing begins to unfurl.

Family Portrait at the Rehab Center

My nurse says, *this is your family,*
scanning the faces behind me

that hover like flies.
Namaste. She bows.

I twist plastic beads
around a strip of leather on my wrist.

When my mother
lays her head on my chest,

I remember the black horse
that nuzzled me there.

They visit each Sunday.
They bridle their worry,

the bit metalling every word.
And after the horses we drink tea.

I notice my hand, which has begun
to drip blood down my white jeans.

How am I this far from myself?
It seems I'm always apologizing

to tongue depressors, little wooden posts
to fence the stampede in my veins.

A stable of monsters, I say,
knowing there is only me.

The Spirit Change

Not a soul must ever know.

Mom's black hair a wing in pool light,
her glass of wine a big red eye. Drinking
in the lounge chair, head thrown back.
Drinking in the sky with her moonless eyes.
Little bottles in the closet, always hiding.
Always hiding under sheets like jewels.
I was looking in the closet; I was looking
out the blinds. Mom taking out the trash
that jangled. Mom's bags full of storm chimes.
I wanted to touch the ghost of her face,
but the face was under water now,
eyes like buoys bobbing on meniscus,
eyes like the eyes in the water below.

～

No doubt the universe had a "first cause" of some sort, the God of the Atom, maybe, hot and cold by turns.

worst frost in years
exist exist
and her mother
grafting
the purple fruit
myself
sweet to see
away
my shears
God
in the fruit

—

sickness no
no new system
and her mother
does not
in sun
when I was young
my own work
I am only
my God
the center
wine

keep growing down
I am her
grafting
make old vines new
how I want
how I
the ripening fruit
as young as
my science
in the bedrock
ripening

rootstock
mother
does not heal
O how I want
to remember
want to be
I cut myself
my roots
my genesis
a stirring
on my tongue

The philosophy of self-sufficiency is not paying off.

Mom? No answer. *Mom?*
Her hands were clamped as bivalves

when she pulled over on a thin strip of shoulder
and the white minivan became a submarine.

She couldn't breathe and I felt
all the pressure of being her child.

She wrung her hands—a strange, arthritic prayer.
I opened the sliding door

and edged around the side of the van,
waving my hands above my head, blasts

of wind from passing cars nearly
knocking me down. A man in a tan Toyota

pulled over. I don't know what they said
to each other, but then he was driving

us home. Mom put her head
between her knees. She breathed.

I understood her fear was imagined.
Later, she called that man an angel.

Later that year I turned my back on God.

~

Then, and only then, do we become as
open-minded to conviction and as willing
to listen as the dying can be.

Before I told my mother
I was no longer her daughter,
a worm crawled into my ear.
It spoke in her voice. *Whore,*
it whispered. So I smoked a joint
on the dorm roof and lit
a Mary candle. My tongues
were in pentameter. My tongues
were learned at Jesus camp,
where men hung
themselves on the cross
and told me my body was bad,
where I'd learned to live
without her. I thought
I could control myself. Then
the sky became my roof
and the floor was scrawled
in devotionals I'd learned
but still don't understand.
From that high,
myself was very far away.

—

It was only by repeated humiliations that we were forced to learn something about humility.

I was humiliated because I was weak and the man's gun was on my face and it was my fault we were there in the first place. I took the car with K. because we wanted chasers. It wasn't my car, it was my best friend's car and it was her birthday. We got some cokes at 7-Eleven then parked behind the strip club with its retro-Vegas orange-red sign glinting LIPSTICK in the neon boneyard of Harry Hines Avenue. We rolled the windows down, took some shots, followed them with sips of soda. The first man held his gun like it was his own finger against K.'s forehead. The second man held his gun like a telescope, its black barrel an aperture against my hair. The first man said to turn off the car. K. began to whine and I unclasped my silver necklace. They could have kept us in the car. They could have done anything they wanted. Then the car was gone. We were alone again, crouched in the parking lot behind someone's Honda. When my dad came to pick us up I saw that against the steering wheel his hands were shaking. Then he said how stupid we were. I still have not forgiven him for this, the truth.

⁓

. . . in other moments, we found ourselves thinking,
when enchanted by a starlit night, "Who, then, made
all this?" There was a feeling of awe and wonder,
but it was fleeting and soon lost.

Mom had been sober a year.

On a family trip, everyone else
drinking, she slipped

in a pool of wine—the entire bottle

broken and spilled, discarded.
How angry she must have been

swimming in the pool of what
seemed like her own blood.

One can be smart about storing wine.

If you keep it in the darkest corner
it might survive. When you open it,

let a little air in. Like my mother's

kitchen in the mornings,
all light blue and yellow,

papered in cheerfulness. Her hair

pulled back, her jawline smooth.
Sometimes the air toughens the wine,

gives it that rustic flair.

But we can't change what we inherit.
The flaw is forever.

⁓

We will want to rest on our laurels.

Do not go to your mind
for a solution. The mind
is what tells us

little fucked-up stories
and then we reach again
for the wine.

As when she relapsed
at the football party
and was sent home alone.

My sister and I did not live
at home anymore, so it was
just my brother and Dad.

When they came home
there she was on the basement stairs.
My brother remembers this well:

he checked her pulse.
The next day they checked her in.

—

It is a spiritual axiom that every time we are disturbed,
no matter what the cause, there is something wrong with us.

Before Mom could see, light was a horse on fire.
But she remembered Muybridge, the Horse in Motion,

the Pegasus moment—all four legs in flight.
A body can become instantly myth,

and the horse, like a candle, was blown out.
Twelve years since her last drink and still

her vision blurs, and still I worry over my own gray line.
It isn't easy to breathe under all this smoke.

Always a thirst in the pit of the mind.
Always the galloping. Always the late nights.

While he was proving that horses could fly,
Muybridge shot a man, fled to Guatemala,

and got away with it. There are many ways
a body can take flight.

—

What we must recognize now is that we exult
in some of our defects. We really love them.

When I went to my first AA meeting
everyone smelled like smoke

which I liked and I couldn't take my eyes
off a girl with a blue streak

in her hair thinking how easily
one small bond could break

and I would be her; she,
my only window into this room

of downturned faces, stale coffee.
Mom was getting her five-year chip.

When she stood up
I saw her.

It was not her
and the most her

I'd ever seen.
All the faces moved

in a collective gesture
of recognition, not pity,

under her face that lit
like a moon the carpeted room.

iii.

Epistle from the Hospital for Gaslighting

to E.P.

OPEN WIDE the poet says
when I sit on his examining table
to tell him where it hurts.
He saved me from my marriage,
he tells me, and now I am locked
in this room on the hospital's top floor,
nowhere for my blonde braid to fall
but in my own hands.
YOU'RE INSANE, he says.
I try to answer, but my words are flies
whose wings he bone-drills
to the walls. He marches down the hall
with his chart, diagnosing
all the women on the floor: bitches all!
Hysterical! Too much in the brain!

She may have a hundred degrees
the poet writes on his prescription pad,
but she is still a stupid, stupid girl.
I fidget on the table, my paper gown
falling open everywhere.
I am weighed for the thousandth time
and the hollow model of a uterus falls
from his desk and clatters like a downed cicada.
Someone hand him the orbitoclast.
Let him silence the buzzing in my head.

Epistle from the Hospital for Harassment

to B.L.

As in a house of mourning / cover the mirrors / Save yourself from yourself / Open the windows / Feed your history to the night / Do not wrestle / against your story / let it keep happening / then kill it—/ the poet who invited you for coffee / a manila folder of poems / meticulously typed / and tucked beneath your arm / all those beats and breaks / silenced / as he thrust his hand on your hip, saying Sweetheart, try your hair in a bun / and What about glasses / If you wore glasses men wouldn't notice you so much / Or your colleague who poked / a bruise on your thigh / guessing at its origins / Or the man who made the bruise / Honey, you're not as stupid as you look—/ Cast it out / until the night is so full of the feathers of your thoughts / it grows the giant wings of a crow / takes off—/ Now lie before the curtained mirrors / Forget what you look like / For better is a wandering eye / than the two you clench shut / waiting for him to finish

Portrait of Demogorgon as Poet

The prince of demons attends a writers' conference.
He travels all the way from the 88th abyss to some woods
in America. The prince of demons doesn't forget his weed
and his condoms, which are only for show—
he plans to impregnate everyone. He is workshopping
his poem about Ferguson, which he heard about on human TV.
The prince of demons' perspective on this matter is very important
because hate makes him blush in a good way. Anyway
his poem has a megaphone so he hears nothing
but his own voice. His poem makes the workshop feel afraid.
To avoid a violent flaying, *not* critiquing the prince
of demons' poems is advised. In his one mind,
the prince of demons wants so badly to be good,
or at least *liked,* but a softie monster never got anywhere,
as his father the king used to say. At the craft lecture,
the prince of demons doodles little drawings of lightbulbs
and naked women. He sits mostly alone at dinner,
shaking his head, chuckling to himself, face unfurling
like a corpse flower, exposing his many sharp teeth.
Fools, he thinks, *all of them fools!* Don't they know
Voltaire named him creator of Earth, that Milton
dreaded him, that he *is* Melville's white whale,
that his very name is taboo? He cries like a man-goat
and closes his face as a fist. There there, demon prince.
It's not your fault. It is we who opened the portal,
who brought you here in the first place.
It's because we worshipped you that you grew so strong.

Giant Squid as Emblematic Feminist

My eyes outsize your wedding china.
I wear my illusion as a cloak. You want to see
all of me? Your silence will unveil
my silver light. The sperm whale: the only one
who can swallow me whole. He wears
my teasing beak as an ornament,
will never unfeel me, never know the lonely
unwrapping of my circled hug. When I wave
to the scientists in their bubble, they say
fan dance, but no, my sway is divination,
the awakening of moon, of carnal light.
Did you know I hold my eggs in my arms?
Did you know, when I let fall the closed blooms
of my tentacles, I am the same shape
as your womb? That I am the mantle
illuminating your face in awe? That I
am a mirror through which you see the face
of the female scientist who discovered me.
That when you see her face, you'll see your own.
Dissect me. You'll find an inkwell there.
Stop looking ahead. Look further down.

Self-Portrait as Nothing

When I give up everything I meet myself again On the mountain's blue slope
The Ozarks Where I used to pray There is at most one empty world Where
the White River cuts through Where I learned black oak To read a snake's

colors   To eat the lemony
ribbon It read Gentle of
showed no one   No one
I don't want to say I am
have tried to fill the body
hands Of whiskey I have
With a man's love Which
impossible But someone
yes I learned the empty world

bodies of ants I wore a pink
Spirit Tender of Heart I
could see me Or the ribbon
disappointed in myself I
Full of leaves Of invisible
learned to sublimate God
is impossible Cruel and
said the only answer to no is
I learned the rivers I learned the

trees I learned to live inside the trees Though I have kept my gentleness secret
I have found nothing In the shape of nothing One can prove only what exists
As in shadows or holes What is immaterial As in forgiveness Which I cannot find

Epistle from the Funambulist Hospital for Invisibility

for P.N.

there is a fine line between looking and not looking
the gaze in its violent shimmering—a knife in the grass—
you, the knife in the grass unseen
this hospital is ribboned with tightropes
we are learning to walk with closed eyes
the other version of you (the one called frances)
stands before her bedroom mirror in a long gone time
duct-taping her sixth-grade breasts flat
dreading the names she would otherwise be called
juggling her hundred mean and prepubescent nicknames
the elephant she thought she was parading through fire
now at the cocktail party of present tense
you ghost through a crowd sometimes you are made of air
night walks through you what are you
what are you everyone asks
seeing, not seeing which is to say we are learning
not to be seen this is what happens
when you leave the center of your own universe
and standing out there on the ring of possibility
look the first version of you dead in the eyes
and without judgment love her

Self-Portrait as Penelope

I wake to someone standing at the edge
        of the bed. It isn't you.
                You are breathing
like a tide beside me. No—
        you have been gone these ten years
and I wake to no breath.
             When finally the sun
          soaks the room in gold, only
my own breath—   distant as a wave
        from a hundred fathoms down.
              How am I this small?
How have I stayed with you   this long
          a tiny blue velella
      gripping your ship's stern
           through foreign water.
Last night   in the gunroom of my mind
          the hall was full
     of my twenty geese
heaped as dead leaves
      their necks broken.
And you   my husband   had broken them.
        See what feathered ruin
          swells around us? I loved
to feed the birds   when I grew
      tired of waiting for you.   How many times
      a winged thing has saved me
        from a knife. Here is the puzzle:
     in the dream
     you killed my pets because you loved me
        and because they were only symbols—
Every time
       you turned your head
you meant something else.
        The gesture, lost on me.

In your disguise, as you watched

                    how long I would wait for you

I knew it was you the whole time.   And yet
              there is a gate through which
              my strange dreams come.

Apology

That was the year of a thousand Mardi Gras.
         The year we stood on the quad
               in the green rain of stinging caterpillars.

Year the trees tossed their wigs of Spanish moss.
         Year we read Lorca
         and imagined our own blood
              wedding. Year we spoke Spanish
in dreams—
         mi amor, you loved me so well.
         What is wrong with me:
that question that turned my tongue to stone.

A thousand poems on your breath:
                    I inhaled you.
A thousand edible flowers: I ate you right up.

         O my love, *es mi culpa, la cagué.*
I still sing to you,
         though I have not seen you in years.

Year of the live oak that rooted in my toes,
         branched between my legs,
         wrapped its fingers
             around the tinderbox of my heart
which I closed
against your knocking.

The year of all the wrong people,
         of saying sorry for all the wrong things,
              year of fault, year I blamed only myself

for the frat party, where you drank until
         you could not see, until I could not see,
              until I could not see you,
         until I could not see myself and
         O god

you did love me well.

When the other boy took me upstairs—
                if I squint I can almost see him—
                I walked of my own volition.
        The night was full of your eyes.

        And when
I stumbled down the stairs again, when I refused
                to know what I knew had just happened,

when I vomited on the street
        and drove home, your eyes
                were the night I slept in
                then and for so many years.

I thought I knew what you saw: a girl
who would always hurt you.
                        In class that Monday,
you wouldn't look at me.
        You never looked at me again.

        Even if you had, I wouldn't
                have seen myself,
        though you loved me, so well—
and for that, and nothing else, I am sorry.

In Which Ophelia Reopens the Box of Hamlet's Drawings

With him, it was always some half-baked
threat, some semi-lucid dream, she says,
palming her own charcoaled jaw
like a prophet. Those were the days I hated

my mother, my friends, my therapist—
anyone who faked listening.
The night's quiet opens like a seafloor fault.
She doesn't want to talk about

the time she tried to die. I wanted him
to love me like lavender, she says, like fennel
and rue. Wanted to curtain myself
with language. When Ophelia speaks

the mind does not ghost into vapor,
but clears, the way lights cut fog
on a drive through the trees. Her anger
achingly sharp, chin like a periscope, the fact

of her like the pinprick of a morning planet.
Her body so light it is hydrogen, her mind a penciled
nucleus. The best likeness: her living. The authentic,
stippled image of a woman, her refusal.

Epistle from the Hospital for Limerence

to K.N.

My friend asks, Do you think a mountain can love you back? We are driving into Colorado where the plains begin to buckle then triangulate and the lack of air starts to go to your head. What she means is not think but believe, not mountain but person, not love but a kind of parallel infatuation. Letters from them like sealed multiverses. Letters in which your life is not yours. Letters like one-dimensional strings in which you pull a thread and unravel a semblance of your old self. That particular relief. Limerence lasts longer than romantic love but not as long as a healthy partnership. I thought healthy partnerships were supposed to involve romantic love. I thought a lot of things. Driving into the mountains, I know I will not see the man who called me bitch. Who called me stupid. Who called me child, who I think I still love. I project his face onto the flatirons. I project his face onto the salted streets, onto the coffee shop window until I remember: Vasopressin. Oxytocin. My body's clingy chemicals. My friend says with her eyes: don't trust it. *Believe her,* I tell myself now, shouting across the distance of this poem. Believe her!

Ophelia Meets Demogorgon

Dress still dripping, Ophelia rocks in a white wood chair
at the roadside diner, counting all her vengeances,
there's fennel for you, and columbines . . . a-down a-down, she chuckles.
She enjoys a good gin cocktail, takes the stones from her pockets,
arranges them in a star at her feet. She's alone. It's delicious.
In the trees she hears some rustling and a face like a flower emerges—
a face she's never seen before (something for her collection, she thinks).
This reptilian bloom-face, attached to a lithe, man-like body,
saunters toward her as an insect on its wiry legs.
She is not afraid, woods glazed in a gimlet haze,
and the worst, she thinks, is behind her. The petals of his face
fold back and there is something wondrous in all those shining teeth,
in all those ligaments and ribs. A large black lightning
cloud descends over the woods and Demogorgon
kneels before her, picks up a stone, and swallows it whole.
This deference, this act resembling knightly duty, excites her.

Ending the Affair at the Garden of Earthly Delights

> Happiness is like glass; it soon breaks.
> —FLEMISH PROVERB

Left

I visit the Prado three times in one week, spend hours circling
Bosch's panel, turning the ring he gave me over and over
in my right hand, gold already worn, the cubic zirconia
glinting dully like molars in the museum's white light.

What callous monsters crawl from the pond with their slithering
amphibious tails and their thousand multiplying cilia.
I am tempted toward cruel people, drunk on my own
capacity for forgiveness. For weeks, he offered me

handfuls of fruit until I bit. Once in the dark, pinned
beneath his body, I heard him say *I will never let you go—*
do you hear me? Eve with her wrist in the vise of her father.
Eve with her bird bones, Eve without Adam.

Eve who cannot even touch her own ground.
Eve in the shadow of all the pale animals, Eve
who is always hungry. And Eve, when you're always hungry,
I know, chances are you'll pick from the wrong tree.

Center

Chaos of all the bodies
in this world. So many of them
cruel, so many of them driven
feverish by the giant red fruit
of the body, huddled and pyretic,
red-hot, picking seeds
from their teeth. Remember this,
I tell myself: there is always
a serpent in the water.

Right

There he is again, in the mussel shell.
Legs sticking out: the muscle of the tongue.
Skin ridged. Black and iridescent
coffin-lid of his narcissism, closing—

And when his mood darkened,
the houses in his brain caught fire.
I tried and failed to lift the knife
from between his ears, which severed
his ability to listen.

Now I am fastened here in the hell
we built for ourselves, dreaming
of finned things that dive beneath
the surface of the mind, that breathe
entire worlds into the brain, which open
and close at the slap of a single white hand.

Epistle from Madrid

to B.B.

Yesterday I saw a man hit by a car, his body
like a newspaper in the street. There are days

when I do not know if I live, though I think I do
and I should be grateful. Most days I am grateful,

very much, like today when I saw *Guernica* during siesta
so no one but me and the guard stood there,

looking. I'm sure everyone says this, but the light
in the painting is an eye; it is also a woman

and the woman with the lamp could be my mother.
I recognize that dread. But I remember

I am lucky. My mother is safe. That woman saw
her town leveled on market day, all her people gone.

Actually, I don't know what she saw but her image
was part of the revolution and she was a torch.

I want to say the important thing is her image: the dying
woman. And the child—a bullet in the eye

of what makes us human. *Forget images,*
the man dying before me on Gran Vía says,

the important thing is collective suffering.
The painting in Paris was a rallying cry.

The painting in Madrid was a memory
of that anthem. The man in the street,

a newspaper, reading to himself the headline of his own pain.
I define the shatter inside me, naming

all the little bombs in my blood.

Ashkelon's Grave

In Ashkelon, Israel, archaeologists discovered a mass
grave of over one hundred infants beneath a Roman bathhouse.
The infants appear to have been intentionally killed.

The statues hear the singing
of a hundred golden birds, drowned.

Three entrances to the bathhouse—
the women and slaves entered

through secret stone arches while men
exercised their arms and were bathed.

And the women who worked there
(the women who fell prey to bathing men)

hoped for girls without bodies.
O how our empires sink us.

⌒

Now the archaeologist sweeps the bones
with her hand brush: femurs like small flutes,

rib cages like rabbit traps, the scared, beating
hearts once imprisoned there

vanished into the empire's invisible palimpsest.
She wants to point to a place in the body,

to say *soul,* to animate the small faces,
to give them all names.

She wants to believe these were abortions,
not infanticide, but the bones are too large

and she is dictated by her own twentieth century,
remembering her castor oil, the picketers.

What to do then, with power's shivering fragments?
She'll warm them. Even the past can feel

a woman's large hands,
its lost teeth like money in her hands.

iv.

Loving Ophelia Is

loving a ghost and loving a ghost is loving yourself
and loving yourself is a sudden sorrow
and a sudden sorrow is the place where the river pools
and the place where the river pools is not suicide and
not suicide is confronting the unknown and confronting
the unknown is the active condition of womanhood
and the active condition of womanhood is the beauteous nature
of Denmark and the beauteous nature of Denmark is lovesickness
and lovesickness is obsession with a version of yourself
and obsession with a version of yourself is egomania and egomania
is a room of mirrors and a room of mirrors is love and hate simultaneously
and love and hate simultaneously is the trick of abuse
and the trick of abuse is a vexation of the mind and
a vexation of the mind is the feeble dawn of gaslight and tea
and the feeble dawn of gaslight and tea is an overbearing husband
and an overbearing husband is a soliloquy of clichés and a soliloquy
of clichés is the misery of scholars and the misery of scholars
is an old friend's skull and an old friend's skull is a sudden sorrow
and a sudden sorrow is holding one's breath
and holding one's breath is swimming away and swimming away
is the other shore on which Ophelia has woken

Epistle from the Hospital for Female Apology

to L.T.

We try on faces that are not sorry,
masquerade through neurology, a parade of ghosts.

Our bodiless bodies, draped in snakeskin and vine,
zero-gravity down the corridors, singing revelations,

casting off the shackles of diction—
I was infinite in prison, the one who used to be Mary sings,

Stoplight my sentence . . . Stoplight my sentence . . .
And another: *My salt my husband's strife across my cheek.*

My salt, my salt . . .
My children forsaken from me . . . I am insolent . . .

Sometimes we don't get the words right.
We no longer stitch the letters to our breasts.

At the masquerade's end,
in the hospital courtyard, we bury *I'm sorry*

with the faces we have lost.
We mother them. We lay them to rest.

Now God holds our sins in her hands, the once-preacher
sings, her face a cape of golden feathers.

Our eyes turn into light as we refrain:
Stay their guns. Life our daughters. Unteach our sons.

Gravitron

Before I walked down the aisle,
my almost-stepson asked, *What do we do now?*

I thought he meant life after marriage,
so I meant it when I said *I don't know.*

And I meant it when I stood at the green edge
of the woods with his father, saying

you're scaring me and *I've nothing left to give.*
I meant it when the boy and I danced in the kitchen

making PB&Js. It made us feel a little
better for a little while. I meant it

when I lifted his toddling brother on my shoulders
so we could watch him ride the Tilt-A-Whirl

and bottleneck a metal ring to win
one of the orange fish that eyed me

through the plastic blister of its prison.
Finally leaving them was like that ride

at the fair: my back was against the wall,
the floor dropped out, my stomach gone.

After that, the ground wasn't ground anymore—
I was walking on atmosphere, forgetting

all my fundamentals, that gravity
forces form and shape, that orbits

must evolve, that if two bodies
are attracted to each other, one of them must fall.

Portrait of You as Hyacinthos

I was tired of the city, that oppressive womb.
You spread nets like quilts under leaves,
taught me to twine a trap. Your lyric

silvered the canopy of trees. I turned the gold disc
over and over in my hands. I couldn't help
but hurt you. For a moment, your face eclipsed

the sun, seemed to linger there. I hate the wind,
how it kept blowing, even after you hit the ground.
Your head in my hands. The earth opening itself,

drinking your blood's sweet milk. As bodies
crowning, violet flowers unfurled. A petaled epitaph,
a loosening. A way of seeing what cannot be seen.

Step-

The year before I became a stepmother,
I climbed the levee stairs, fed

the rest of my old self to the river.
That green leviathan shot my clarity like gin.

Impossible to imagine loving a man
with children I don't yet know,

impossible to mother them
through fathoms of the past, impossible

to hear them calling me,
by mistake, *Mom.*

⁓

We struggle together with words, sounding
them out, my stepson and I, perched

on the bed like tightrope walkers.
What words can help

but those that make us smile, words like *narwhal*
and *Jupiter*. He writes in a hand

that reminds me of my own; his bantam words
climb the page. Words with hooves,

words with horns, words without vertigo.
I say an impossible prayer, to undo, to repair.

Tell me how the story ends, he says,
but I do not skip ahead.

I want to see, selfishly, the unfolding
of his face in age, in story.

The Museum of Who We Used to Be

Jenny, I gave you that unhappy / Book that nobody
knows but you / and me . . .

    —JAMES WRIGHT, "The Idea of the Good"

to D.K.

It's too painful to look at the boy's splayed heart
at the mummy exhibit, so you walk out
to the gift shop with your hands in your pockets.

But I can't stop looking at the open ribs,
the boy-heart, a ruby in a white tree,
thinking of a city night long ago,

so cold, you opened
your leather jacket for me, and then
I was wearing something of yours,

my beating chest singing down the street.
I am not the person I used to be.
And yet, you are someone I used to know,

someone I still know.
Jenny light, Jenny darkness. You misremember
a line of our old favorite poem,

and a scalpel of light goes in through my ribs.
The poet invented Jenny,
I once read, after waking alone in the dark.

Different Kinds of Sadness

to E.A.H.

Sometimes a friend can save your life,
as when you drove in from Albuquerque

the day I left the man I thought would kill me.
We went to the train station and sat

among the Beaux Arts pediments and bas-reliefs
having a cocktail called the Manhattan, Kansas.

You brought a package of fresh tortillas,
some butter, some cheese—we'll survive,

the *we* a sort of kindness, a kind of sadness.
The drinks were garnished

with shriveled figs instead of maraschinos,
which was a different kind of sadness.

The station was built in 1914
and no one who can remember 1914 is left.

Your eyes began to time-travel
behind your white-rimmed glasses

and I knew you were thinking about your son.
The lives we have chosen not to live

are enough to fill the whole day's trains
with ghosts and ghosts and ghosts.

But there are also people
who have known you forever,

which is yet another kind of sadness
because you've only just met.

For John

It's not desiring the fall; it's terror of the flames.
—DAVID FOSTER WALLACE

A flame blooms where the bullet
passed through. Always it blooms
as a wild poppy until I begin to forget
your sleepless face. Always the flame
unfurls there above your deafened ear,
opening and closing like a baby's hand.

Our child would be five today.
I dream of driving, and the car
swallows the highway lines
as Lortabs. I arrive at the trailer
where you lived your last months,
the dishes stacked like ammunition,

the music on low. There on the edge
of the bed is our unborn child.
She reaches for me, clenching and unfolding
the blossoms of her pink hands.
I take her in my arms.

I wake. I must leave you here,
must go on living. You remain with her,
who never lived, sleeping in the field
you painted—red poppies, so many poppies,
wild as wind, and red.

Demogorgon Tries Ophelia for Witchcraft

First he plants a rabbit and a hare
then he shaves her
head and strips her bare.
He loves his little ritual of hate
(evil for God's okay
and criminals of late
like princes of demons and men
are safe). Clutching her
locks in his red claw,
he tests the girl
for witch's marks,
finds only freckles, pearls
of her nipples, a scar—
and so performs the needle test,
as witches cannot bleed
or hurt. Finally a spot
on the heel draws no blood
which justifies
our prince-at-large. He declares
an ordeal of water,
drags a cold bald Ophelia
to his barge, ties her down.
They visit the brook
she survived in her heavy
white cloak and her pretty
little flower-crown.
He strings her up
and casts her out,
a fish in reverse. The line breaks.
She wriggles free,
dives way down. So she isn't a witch
but she is gone
the prince's stupid inquest done.

Letter to My New Sister

For P.D.

Abusive? Not him. You were crazy jealous,
berating, while I wielded my brain like a bow.
Consent, he argued, was you sharing his bed.
Divorce, proof I had no heart. All that charisma. See?
everyone loves him. Hear the thunderous applause?
Fear the man who brandishes a black axe,
gaslit, flint until we sparked.
He always knew we deserved it.
I the only letter he spoke.
J—you said, tell me it's not in my head. I'd recall no
kindness. *You gotta earn kindness, baby,* he'd croon.
Let's loosen the hinges of his rage and run;
marry our own lock-windowed
nights with new wisdom—
only sisters can be bound like this in trauma.
P—did I love you before I knew you? Now we ask
questions. I shut up too much, didn't I,
raising his pointed finger against my own temple:
Shoot the mind right out of me.
True, we tested cliffsides
under the mooning face of a man who cried love,
voracious for gilded mirrors he held then shattered.
Wherever you are, I am with you, allied beyond our
ex who thieved even our eyes. Let's excise our ex-selves.
Yes, leave them. Yes, leave him. Un-
zip the monster from his cruel suit and fly.

Ophelia Slays Demogorgon

The dog will have his day, as some dude once said,
and this is it. I return to my brook, pockets full of rue,
wade in until its cold hands cup my ankles, my hips,
my breasts, my neck—til my hair fans around me
like, what else, a fan. This isn't meant to be pretty.
All Ophelia-as-muse, all Ophelia's poetic death.
No one paid me for that. I flip over. This, my astral plane,
the brook my sensory deprivation chamber. I close
my eyes; the water fills my ears. They are not seashells but ears.
I could hold my breath for days.

It is here beneath the water (I do not float) where the world
flips. I cross over. Swimming away from my body like a soul.
Now I walk. Dark the floor slick a sickening sound a wet
tail slapping water. I do not need my hands in the dark.
I have already been dead. Come, monster.
There he is, kissing the child I never had. No, he is stealing
her breath. He infects her. With all my rue I summon
my suicide. The rage definite as an incision. Come, channel.
Come, impossible light. He whines; he curses
my name. I've heard it all before. With my mind I drive
into the monster until he breaks. His body bursts,
hundreds of black, frantic moths. Then, ash.
I am the one who lives.

Epistle from West Texas

to Joni Mitchell

Bones under trees growing soft,
delicious purple of mountain laurel,
mescal beans rubbed on concrete
until they are coals, until they are buried
in my blood, like you—

your voice a mother tongue
that years ago fanned another ember,
opened the wings of my lungs
to loss. *I don't like to look back,* you say.
But you do anyway—who doesn't.

Blue martins swoop southward,
muddy nest-globes house
white worlds of eggs, eggs that hatch
in the heart's feathery mouth.
Scissortails like peach-halves with swords.
Birds that come to me to die. We dive

into old art, the stir of memory,
of self-revision. *Don't give yourself away,*
you said once, still so young. Head full
of water and swim-starving, I listen
as you sing my favorite song

again, after many years. My guts are twists
of silver fins and wands and synapse.
My voice, singing along, is a river passing under
a bridge—still green—though darker now
as it braids the worn stones. I've seen
shadows; I fly forth. I wait for no one.

Vise

A part of you
has been here all along,
                    a witness.
                    Light like song
              through the sieve
              of the five-fingered fig leaf.
An accident on ice.
Your mother's last drink
                    and the chips that fell
                    like gold coins from her eyes.
              The first man who was cruel.
              See him?
The first man who loved you,
who gave you the silver-
                    coated tailfin of a blue whale.
                    The last man. The memory
              of his voice tightening
              its vise around your neck.
You do not have to be perfect.
All thoughts are prayers,
                    you've learned. Listen.
                    Some people will empty
              their cups so you can drink.
              Remember them.
Some will shine a light on your face
in the dark, will see it's you there dying,
                    and disappear, laughing,
                    down the star-gilded streets.
Remember them, too.
Now let them go.

ACKNOWLEDGMENTS

This book would not have been possible were it not for my family and my friends (my chosen family), many of whom are the recipients of the epistolary poems in this collection: Erin Adair-Hodges, Taneum Bambrick, Bruce Bond, Traci Brimhall, F. Douglas Brown, Jamey Molberg Bullard, Caitlin Cowan, Puja Datta, Maia Gil'Adí, Kassi Hester, David Keplinger, Bridget Lowe, Paula Molberg, Patricia No, Kathryn Nuernberger, Elizabeth A. I. Powell, and Leah Tieger.

I'm enormously grateful to the wonderful people at LSU Press, especially MaryKatherine Callaway, James Long, and Catherine L. Kadair, for their hard work and their faith in the book. Thank you to the National Endowment for the Arts, for believing in my work and for the gift of financial support. Thank you to the Sewanee Writers' Conference and the Vermont Studio Center for the gift of time, and my teachers there who guided me through the early stages of this collection (especially Ross Gay and Marilyn Nelson).

I would like to thank the women responsible for the #metoo movement, especially Tarana Burke, for the crucial act of breaking silences, and my students, who challenge and inspire me daily, especially Savannah Bradley, Amanda DeJesús, Maggie McMichael, and Maggie Warren.

And Cameron Seip, thank you for your knowing the music of my heart, for bringing me back to life.

Thank you to the hardworking editors of the following journals and anthologies, where these poems were originally published:

Bear Review: "Self-Portrait as Penelope"
Bellevue Literary Review: "Step-"
Birmingham Poetry Review: "Turbine" and "Epistle from the Funambulist Hospital for Invisibility"
Boulevard: "Ashkelon's Grave" and "For John"
Connotation Press: An Online Artifact: Three sections from "The Spirit Change"
Grabbed Anthology (edited by the Blue Room Collective: Richard Blanco, Cary Moro-Gronlier, Nikki Moustaki, and Elisa Albo): "Said the Poet" and "Epistle from the Hospital for Harassment"
Green Mountain Review: "The List," "Epistle from the Hospital for Laundry," "Said

the Poet," "Abecedarian for Us," "Ophelia Meets Demogorgon," "Ophelia Slays De-
mogorgon," and "Family Portrait at the Rehab Center"

Gulf Coast: "Epistle from the Hospital for Text Messaging"

The Journal: "Epistle from the Hospital for Emily Post's Wedding Gift Return Eti-
quette" and "Epistle from the Hospital for Harassment"

JuxtaProse: "In Which Ophelia Opens the Box of Hamlet's Drawings"

Mississippi Review: "Eating Alone"

Missouri Review Poem of the Week: "Different Kinds of Sadness"

NELLE: "Epistle from West Texas," published as "Self-Portrait as Landscape"

Ninth Letter: "Self-Portrait as Nothing"

Redivider: "Giant Squid as Emblematic Feminist"

Pilgrimage: "The Wolf of Coole Park"

The Pinch: "Vise"

Ploughshares: "Note" and "Epistle from the Hospital for Cheaters"

Poetry International: "Note" (reprint)

Public Pool: "Apology" and "Digital Infinity"

Soundings East (as winner of the Claire Keyes Poetry Prize): "Epistle from the Hospital
for Evolution," "Epistle from the Ruins," "Epistle from Madrid," "Epistle from the
Hospital for Limerence," "Epistle from the 8th Grade," "Epistle in Utero," "Epis-
tle from the Hospital for Gaslighting," and "Epistle from the Hospital for Female
Apology"

Southern Indiana Review: "Hippocampus"

Stirring: A Literary Collection: "Gravitron" and "The Night I Left"

SWWIM (Supporting Women Writers in Miami): "After Pawning the Engagement
Ring"

Tupelo Quarterly: "The Love Song of Demogorgon"

Epigraphs in "The Spirit Change" are taken from *Twelve Steps and Twelve Traditions,*
Alcoholics Anonymous World Services Inc., first published in 1953.

CPSIA information can be obtained
at www.ICGtesting.com
Printed in the USA
LVHW092300170120
644022LV00005B/570